MIXED

EMOTIONS

By

Gerald Mushi
www.soulfreshworld.com
email: gm@soulfreshworld.com

About the Author

Gerald Mushi, specializes in creative writing with a mission, "To help connect souls using Unorthodox Literature". The Nebraska native holds a Bachelor of Science from Middle Tennessee State University with a concentration in Exercise Science. Even more he takes part in various projects that focus on healing his community through poetry.

As a member of the National Association of Black Storytellers, Gerald with over 20 years of experience in writing poetry and music, creates a unique message that leaves a dynamic impact and contribution to his community. His experience and motivation to breed a whole new writing culture, inspired him to write his debut book *Mixed Emotions*.

This book is dedicated to the
great mothers, falling soldiers, and friends
that lived amongst me and
the universe:

Bibi (Grandma)
Both my Babu(s) (Grandpops)
Victor Parham (falling soldier/brother from another)
Demetric Peebles (falling soldier/brother from another)
Ky'Andreas Caphart (great mother and friend)
Poison Ivy (falling soldier)
Ramadan Shabazz (falling soldier)
Charles L. Mctorry (mentor and father figure)
Jay Johnson (falling soldier)
Bookie (falling soldier)
Corey Frye (falling soldier)
Maria (friend)
Ashley Homertz (friend)
Chase Harris (falling soldier)

???What is Unorthodox Literature???

un·or·tho·dox
ˌən'ôrTHəˌdäks/

adjective

adjective: unorthodox

contrary to what is usual, traditional, or accepted; not orthodox.
"he frequently upset other scholars with his unorthodox views"

synonyms: unconventional, unusual, radical, nonconformist, avant-
garde, eccentric, maverick, strange, idiosyncratic; More

antonyms: conventional

Gerald Mushi's definition:

Unorthodox Literature is the direct line of communication and thought whether it's grammatically
correct or not. When people communicate in this modern world, the only thing that matters is did
you simply get the message? There's the "yes" and you got the over explained 20 word "yes..."
People are running out of time and want to get straight to the point in as little time possible. Slang is
not shunned anymore. People want the raw truth now. If school systems are failing our language
would be a part of the plummet too. So, I start my journey to encourage others to not be scared to
express themselves in their own way. The more we share our visions and views, the more we learn as
a human race.

WARNING

This book contains explicit language not suitable for children under the age of 18. Mature audience only. Not a traditional style of literature. Open your mind. Enjoy!

Impossible

Thoughts of reaching impossible

The distance seems astronomical

Feels like a whole lifetime taking it step by step,

Impatient choices introduce lessons of regret

Depression starts winning as you lose all respect

Failing to see time in the mirror whenever it reflects,

Instead seeing disappointment, where did my confidence go?

Losing the appetite for accomplishing goals

Seeking alternative routes to heal my soul

Has made the wheel harder to grip with control, CRASH!

Damn was that worth it? You realized you not perfect

Forgot your purpose behind feeling worthless, well deserve is…

Earned from countless hours, ten thousand to be exact,

Move far away from failure to a successful habitat

Adapt to surprises and obstacles when they knock

Answer door with optimism and all positive thoughts

Discover what's impossible is absolutely NOT!!!

Intercourse Café

Nothing is like a good morning appetite

My bread is brick like three times in toaster,

You've been brewing like coffee all thru the night

I'm excited to have a taste of your Folders,

I spread you like jelly, butter, or cream cheese

Climb your tree for that soft forbidden fruit,

Put banana in your blender, make a great smoothie

The blacker the berry the sweeter the juice,

We leave for work and meet up later for lunch

A spicy break hotter than Cheyenne,

Love when you season my meat and have a munch

I dip into your sauce until I bust cool ranch,

Times up, clock in, back until off work

Dinner with you will be special,

Can't wait to eat your sweet caramel dessert

And fold you like a pretzel,

Just an appetizer before main dish

Simmering together this recipe I'm lovin,

Also love the fact you don't smell like fish

We better slow down before there's a bun in oven...

Pride

Too much to listen

Too much to understand

No room for you and me

So please change your plans,

Go the other way because my way is right

I'm too stubborn to believe you want to help my life,

I'll do it on my own no worries I got it

Running with the world on my shoulders like I can't get exhausted,

If I do I won't mention for my pride won't allow it

Will I ever admit I'm wrong one day I seriously doubt it!

All you want to do is help, all I want to do is lead

You go out your way to find the answer but I say let me be

Why are you still here? What is it you see?

It's obvious my pride will eventually kill me.

Beautiful Creature

Sweet innocent beauty you have my full attention
I adore you truly just thought I would mention,
The person you are is beyond comprehension
All your beauty is concealing your cruelest intentions,
You steal hearts for a living
Know just how to attract a man
You allow him to rush
Play along with his plans,
Give him your privacy she uses hers as a tool
To manipulate and get what you want from this fool,
Working hard to keep you
She can't wait til you leave to
Reveal the creature inside
Her disguise unbelievable,
Her eyes turn red then her horns come out
This isn't the goddess you left staying at your house,
This woman is different this one loves the lies
The lust the thrills of capturing good guys,
He's so proud of his trophy little he knows she
Is hiding behind a smile much better then emoji,
No concerns about you she just agrees and repeats
She has no intention to get close in her mind you're history,
Men think you gullible thinking with the wrong head
Mysterious how them same men are tangled in her web,
She's magnetic when she walks even passing cars turn heads
She's been known to get husbands to lay in other beds,
No woman likes her, but she no longer cares
It boost her confidence to continue playing unfair,
"It's your mans fault!" is her favorite excuse
She accepts the role of mistress for so many dudes,
Why you not valuing yourself? You are more than you display
She said everything changed when her Uncle raped her back in the day.

Rage

Fuck you let's go feeling furious not nice

I can use hands, ammunition, and Swiss Army knife

Civilized turned serial overnight

I'm a fireball ready to burn what's in sight

My thermometer busted, I'm not tryna discuss shit

Past boiling point I'm the wrong one to fuck with,

Tape your mouth you talking too much

Put plastic bag over your head and cover it up,

Squeeze tight…wait patiently until you stop breathin

You'll think twice bout fuckin with good people for no reason

Steppin on my toes until I finally respond

Ignoring my peaceful words leads to bodily harm,

I want you to see the spark coming from my firearm

Guaranteed this the last light you'll ever turn on,

Excuse my rage "HELL NO!" You deserve this torture

No remorse for those who take from hard workers

Should my frustrations be justified by commitin murder?

I'll worry bout that later as I stab you over and over.

Sewer Suites

Welcome to sewer hotel
Please excuse all smells
Majority visits end up with death or jail,
People come all the time, reserve rooms drop of a dime
Responsibilities left behind, to check in a room for the blind,
Not blind from vision but blind from reality
This popular tour site makes people leave their family,
Make a conscious person plead insanity
Tryna justify hitting two parked cars in wife's Camry,
Guard your belongings the cameras be
Off....No recording at Sewer suites
Cops are here heavily, because nothing here heavenly
Most elevators go up, here it's the opposite,
Further down the suites get more luxurious but ignore how hot you get,
Warning signs everywhere to let you know you're unsafe
But deception is the best way to define this place,
People come and don't leave til they've lost hair and teeth
Death toll at 83 and that's only last week,
No exercise room but this is where you come to run
Away from the world, throw away all you've become,
Both grown and young, all ages are welcome
To explore all the toxins some deadly like venom,
People wanna leave but stay, no judge can keep them away
Probation definitely don't stop this hotel paaarrrtaayyy!
Aaaayyyyy!!!! Everyone smiling and stumbling
Barely can understand people because the drugs got them mumbling,
11 people had seizures still people happy to be here
Up 74 hours, yes, human zombies you'll see here,
Ambulance sirens are muted because overdosing is light
Bring them back to life, crazy enough they'll stay another night,
Overdraft for overnight is a common sacrifice
Here you see mothers leaving their newborns to get back to their vice,
Why not call it quits and give up this harmful place?
Sewer Suites is my addiction I've been tryna escape!

Let it go!!!

Wanna Know Ask the Source

Rumors are the watered-down truth
Gossip is passed along without a clue
Running your mouth when it should be glued
Because only the source knows the news

Jive is all talk nothing solid
Lies are stories that are polished
You might as well listen to an alcoholic
If you're not going to the source for knowledge

Need to know exactly what it cost?
Third party like to rip off
If you spent more it's not my fault
Because the source knows it all

Wanna know why they ignore you?
Working hard but don't reward you?
There's no answers anyone else can assure you
Because only the source knew before you

She left you or he left her?
All the pointed fingers in a pot to stir
Both get the scoop from close friend they prefer
But the source would've helped both from becoming insecure.

Who Got Who?

You were so perfect at first, had me blinded by your layers

You never knew I was a jerk, even worse smooth operator,

Both our phones on lock, acting like we trust each other

When I check mine you watch, corner of your eye can be clever,

You gave me your heart, I was too arrogant to keep it

You was loyal from the start, until you found out my secrets,

Can't blame you for your actions, I'm the reason you insecure

Women hint before it happens, saying they not comfortable here,

That's your stop sign, red light, proceed at your own risk

Silly thinking "yeah right" my girl not capable of this,

Ignorant me women are better at this game we call cheatin

They can change like the weather and hurt you more getting even,

I slid off with a random, you opened up to my hommie,

Honestly never imagined, the broken heart you would show me,

You do dirt out of spite, I fuck off cuz I'm drunk,

At the end of the night, its a weak excuse you not dumb,

You gave chance after chance, selfishly took it for granted

Damn I miss holdin hands, we used to be so romantic

Now that the damage is done, you helped me respect women more,

You're not an object for fun, sorry for being IMMATURE.

Caged Animals

Captured from the wilderness cuffs cover our wrist
Put us in a cage can't believe this still exists
One person makes decision of how long we shall live
In this controlled environment for a private profit
At nighttime you hear keys from a scared walking guard
Look them dead in the eye you can see they've been scarred
Picked on as a child give em a badge give em charge
Watch em all abuse their power hiding behind the law
We lose our names to our mothers to be called inmates
They ship us here and there label that intake
Strip us tell us squat and don't forget to cough
Keep property and hand us cheap cloths that taxpayers bought
How is it ok to keep 90 people in one room?
Give us breakfast during the moon, dinner early afternoon
Junkies, rapists, dealers, scammers, and goons
Mixed with the innocent, the brilliant, and the coming home soon
Keep in mind I said 90 is 4 toilets enough?
2 urinals and 6 showers no curtains to cover up
No stall doors so we have to shit in front of each other
Feed us processed foods so all our stomachs will suffer
Give us the run around every time we have questions
Send us to the hole for releasing aggression
Time moves slow feel like an hour when only seconds
Guards keep disrespectin cuz they know we have no weapons
Give us thin blankets then freeze us thru the night
We wash our own draws, hang on bunk til dried
Next to the wet towel, socks, and t-shirt on the side
Ever wonder why an inmate decides suicide?
There's a such thing as you can think too much
In a room full of negative energy, it's positive to blow up
Almost everyday there is a fight, got us turning on us
When we should all team up, unite, and free all of us!

2 Unfair

I give you 2, you give me one
I extend my arms, you give me thumbs,
I brought a loaf, you bring me crumbs
I'm down to some, you come with none,
I pay for 2, you say thanks
When it's your turn, complain you can't,
Seems like your issues are always bigger
Bring out violin cry me a river,
I don't have 2, only have 1
But you'll take my last leave me none,
Countin on me 2 always have it
I worked for this, don't know magic
Took 2 jobs 2 make this all appear
While you job hoping every year
Stick with one then get another
Gonna take 2, 2 get out the gutter.

CrusHHH

Smiling more than normal
My speech all of sudden formal,
I don't want to fumble a word
and be another kicked to the curb,
I sure know a woman's worth
And you're soaring above superb,
No lie your beauty got me nervous
First impression has to be perfect,
My confidence better be thru the roof
Don't come off too cocky or else poofff!
Can't wow you with jewels like you last couple approachs
Nothing new to hear brag, you used to the boasts
I'm sure you're tired of free meals and the fanciest toasts
I'm just gonna be me I'm sure you'll love that the most,
You got me talking to myself that's how wonderful you are
Out the whole entire galaxy you're the brightest star,
You similar to the sun get too close I will melt
There's not enough fresh roses to express myself,
When you spoke, I froze up forgot all that I practiced
Everything I rehearsed for the moment had vanished,
Never panic keep cool, introduced myself how are you?
Like a gentleman shook her hand and thought damn her skin smooth,
I've been hearing god is a woman I believe that is true
I feel like elementary school the crush I have for you!

Depressed

Feeling of nothingness empty inside

My heart and an axe collide

Wanna run but my stide

Isn't long enough to escape

The reality of fate can feel like a blade,

Sharp slice thru my soul

Penetrating thick skull

Not a trace of blood but this cut painful,

Feeling weak, losing sleep, short when I speak

Canceling activities lacking the energy

I just wanna leave…this world not for me,

Seem like nobody's there now I no longer care

I feel more underneath than the Hanes I wear,

Complain life unfair blaming everyone else

People wanna help but I'm ashamed of myself,

Where were you at first? Answer my angry question

I'm not tryna hear everything alright & count your blessings

Just need you to solve my problems so I won't be aggressive

But the problem is ME I'm suffering from depression…

(OWN UP TO YOURSELF)

Private Eye Public Eye

No one knows who you are

Only you can display it

Basic, complaisant, you'll never say it,

Ugly inside but you lie behind the truth

Attack others because the one you hate is you,

So friendly but friendly fire more like it,

Dark inside but you come off enlightened,

What happens in private is behind closed doors

The public eye can't see what's under the floor,

The private eye has seen unsolved stories

Public eye can only prove thru laboratories,

Stealth is to be private in the public eye

Sometimes public eye has to be private eye

In fear that the private eye may retaliate

For helping other public eyes investigate,

Secrets in private by any means can't go public

To remain a saint in public requires a private budget

Lost Souls

Immortal soul how can you be lost?
Where did the confusion come from?
You was once reaching for the top
Think how many things you've done done

If they've worked you would be in a better place
Not feeling like you are now
All the years seem like a waste
Looking back to moments you felt proud

To be alive feeling you have a purpose
All the energy in the world
To try whatever you worship
Influenced by diamond and pearl

Mama told you they're not real
But you had to see for yourself
Seeing her struggle with bills
Fueled your desire for wealth

All the gifts she failed getting
Helped play a role with your conscious
As a kid you don't want to be the kidding
All the jokes of having non cents

Make something happen quick
Most walk thru the first open door
Most regret that option picked
Hell naw not doing dat no more

Question a role model
Apply some of their answers
To your own life and follow
Their footsteps could be cancerous

What's the chase about?
Mama said patience is a virtue
Not all suppose to take same route
Sucks finding out following could hurt u

Paradise

Your face as I enter
Your eyes as you sit
Love how you feel
Slow turn the faucet
Soft turn to solid
Sixty four hydraulics
Add 5 to the number
Whose on top whose under?
Experiment like science
Are you as crazy as I am?
We speak using tongue
When I talk her eyes close,
As your body goes numb
Start the firework show
Paradise such a wonderful place to be
Fall asleep looks like someone poured water on sheets...

Pray and Pray on My Downfall

Success brings the worst out of your crabs
Holding on to your legs with dead weight,
They always remind you of the past
Bringing up moments they went out their way,

To be there or do something so small you forgot
Or they just ride the wave of calling you a friend,
Their life is over so hang on to what you got
They'll vice grip hold onto you til the end,

The end is realization of you using me
All the "yes man" answers had me blinded,
Now that I've said no your not true to me
All of sudden I've lost my kindness?

Gotta grow up sometime, take on more assignments
You having troubles with adulting,
Now some my friends turn conniving
It's the progress whose faulting

To keep bond strong when I had less we was cool
I try to encourage but you don't wanna hear,
Say I'm actin better than you
I never said stay in the rear???

All your excuses keep you down
Say your struggle is much harder,
To me you're a clown
You never took life farther,

Now you want to laugh at my mistakes
Because you can't afford to make any,
Borrowing money and don't repay
Because you feel I got plenty,

Did nothing to receive the fruit of my labor
I cut you off now my best friend becomes hater
My downfall would answer all of your prayers
Keep praying because I'm not even stopping for thy maker!

Any last words...

You was leader you were chosen
You helped my soul when it was broken
You was around first time smokin
Tough love we was always jokin,
Striving to get more, planning like pinky and the brain
Driving at an early age, pawn cars from dope game
Thanks to your Unk for putting up that cocaine
I was 14 got pulled over they searched everythang,
He saved me from a real charge, juvenile let me go
I remember playing Juvenile when moms let ya drive to the sto,
You rapped so much it made me give it a shot
Makin videos you wanted to be neighborhood hot,
Remember getting put out 7th grade, trippin that they let us walk???
We went to the sto, then to moms, and grilled hot dogs
We never "snitched" on each other
Treated each other like fam
I knew you came from the Gutta
And I was the poor African
Joke after joke, you was Fat, I talk funny,
Shared one common goal fuck the world get this money,
My bro my bro, hate you passed away
I never got to say what I wanted to say....................................

Acknowledgements

The author wishes to make special mention to recognize the following people:

Imani Mushi, daughter, I love you beautiful!!!
Moms and Pops, I wouldn't be here. Thanks for all your sacrifices.
Both my sisters, Christina and Winnie, Thanks for always being there.
Brothers, Cliff and Tom, Thanks for being inspiring and helping me.
Nephew and nieces, Keep progressing and never stop giving your all.

Mixed Emotions

By Gerald Mushi

Order additional copies at www.amazon.com,
www.barnesandnoble.com and other fine book sellers.

www.soulfreshworld.com

Printed in USA

ISBN: 978-0692063187